ENTERPRISE RESOURCE PLANNING SYSTEMS 2017

12

FREQUENTLY ASKED QUESTIONS ABOUT ENTERPRISE RESOURCE PLANNING SYSTEMS

BRIAN IINUMA
AND
ERIC KLAUSS

Published by Strategic Systems Group, Inc.

ISBN 9780990825272

Copyright © 2017 Strategic Systems Group, Inc.

A special offer for those interested in this book

As a thank you for your interest in our book, we are offering a Free pass to a webinar titled, "Outgrowing QuickBooks and What is Enterprise Resource Planning? In this 60-minute presentation, we'll identify the key indications that you've outgrown your basic accounting system, describe the flow of financial data through an ERP system, and provide an overview of Tier 2 enterprise resource planning applications.

To register, go to http://bit.ly/2iz6qJ7

For Mom and Dad

*Who always encouraged me to do my best, and for Michele,
Daniel, and Michael to whom I am grateful for their love
and support*

Brian

To Mom & Dad

*For the many trips to library and the gifts of reading and
writing, and to Scott & Laura who taught me the meaning
of the words "brother" and "sister"*

Eric

TABLE OF CONTENTS

ABOUT

Have you ever tried to make sense of ERP software and felt that you just got back jargon and acronyms? Are you struggling with an ERP systems implementation and have team members telling you that you've gone down the wrong path? Does it look like your business has been impacted adversely?

Brian Iinuma has over 25 years' IT experience in Enterprise Resource Planning (ERP), payment processing, and direct marketing. He is the President and co-founder of Strategic Systems Group, Inc. (SSG, http://ssgnet.com), a provider of IT services to small and mid-sized manufacturing and distribution companies. SSG's core competence is the implementation and support of ERP applications including Infor LN, Microsoft Dynamics, and SYSPRO. Mr. Iinuma is active in the Southern California chapter of International Association of Microsoft Channel Partners (IAMCP - SoCal) and the Microsoft Community Connections Program (MCC). He has made a series of technology presentations to the South Bay Chambers of Commerce, the Orange County chapter of SCORE, and a number of business associations. Mr. Iinuma is a #1 bestselling author and holds B.S. and MBA degrees from the University of California, Los Angeles.

Eric Klauss has over 20 years of experience selling, consulting and recommending business technology solutions, especially ERP & CRM as a customer, consultant, and salesperson in the industry. Today, he provides his sales and marketing expertise to PartnerSource Solutions (http://www.partnersource-it.com) clients and is a SCORE Mentor to business clients in Southern California. Eric, a #1 bestselling author, currently serves as President of the Southern California chapter of International Association of Microsoft Channel Partners and is the Chairperson for the Microsoft Community Connections team.

INTRODUCTION

"12 Frequently Asked Questions About Enterprise Resource Planning (ERP) Software" was spawned to address the most common questions we receive from executives about their organizations' ERP systems. These questions touch on topics ranging from software selection to implementation to ongoing support issues. In this book, we'll provide answers to 12 frequently asked questions that are likely to represent important issues in your organization and how to address them. Business owners, CEOs, CFOs, I/T executives, and middle managers responsible for sales, operations, and finance may benefit from reading this book.

Each of the following chapters is intended to answer a question about ERP systems and their implementation. In each chapter, there are key concepts that provide additional detail and color.

CHAPTER 1 - SELECTING AN ERP APPLICATION

What factors should a small or medium-sized business consider when selecting an ERP application?

As in many situations, the answer is often "It depends." Often, the type and size of organization and types of business processes are key factors.

Selecting the right software is a critical success factor in an ERP systems implementation. Many organizations face the tough decision of selecting the right ERP application that suits their type of business. In order to select the right ERP software, a number of factors should be considered. These include industry type, size of the organization, manufacturing process, and the level of fit with the existing business processes, infrastructure, and technology.

Industry Type

To obtain relevant information, business owners and executives should ask questions like,

- "What other tools are business organizations using today?"

- "What is the size and nature of the primary business?"
- "Is there a unique vertical solution that addresses the company's largest market?"

If there is a vertical market product that fits the business perfectly, then despite the price difference compared to other solutions, it might be the right application to implement.

Company Size

No matter the size of the business, selecting the right ERP application is one of the most important decisions the executive team can make. When owners and executives realize that the business has outgrown the basic accounting solution it began with or when they find out that they have a lot of disparate Excel spreadsheets and data in silos, then it's time to bring everything together into a single package. These are indications that executives should begin the search for the right ERP software to fit the company's primary manufacturing process.

Different kinds of applications will fit different sorts of companies. Company size is a big determinant of the kind and complexity of application that should be used for the organization. For instance, a small business using

QuickBooks and spreadsheets to run its manufacturing organization will most likely not need a Tier 1 application like SAP or Oracle because it will just be too big for the job. In cases like that, it would make more sense to choose a less complex package, because the leap from QuickBooks and spreadsheets to a Tier 2 or Tier 3 ERP application will be much more likely to succeed.

Fit with Existing Business Processes

Understanding the business process goes a long way towards helping organizations chose the right package. If clients do not have a detailed understanding of the business process and the way it works, they may have a hard time making the right choice. In order to overcome this challenge, team members must analyze the internal processes of the business and detail them all out; this is because regardless of what accounting or ERP solution is selected, the whole point is to bring those processes into the system. So, before making a choice of solution to use, clients must have their arms around the organization's core business process.

The application should be selected such that it fits in with the existing business process, or at least be very close. It is challenging to change the business process and the ERP application at the same time, but in many situations, that is exactly what the company needs to do. The company's executives and team members should review the business' processes and modify and streamline them before selecting an ERP application. If this process is done well, then the company stands a better chance of getting the system implemented.

Manufacturing Process

Manufacturing companies have different challenges so let's discuss those briefly. A company's manufacturing processes will have bearing on what ERP systems would be most suitable. For example, the applications that support process manufacturing could be quite different from those that support make-to-stock, make-to-order, and engineer-to-order operations, which would be radically different from a professional services or retail organization.

Fit with Existing Infrastructure and Technology

For most companies, instead of delving into using an ERP solution because others are using it, it is important to first assess the underlying technology. For instance, for a company using Microsoft Outlook for email and has a lot of data in Excel files, implementing a Microsoft solution or something equally deeply integrated will be a sensible choice.

Organizations need to consider other start-up factors including:

- The underlying infrastructure of the company
- The customer relationship management system currently in use
- Whether or not it should be integrated with the ERP solution in the future

Enterprise Considerations

Just like small and medium-sized organizations, large business enterprises are also faced with the challenge of selecting the right ERP package for their business. For instance, a division that is part of a larger organization, often, will have no choice but to use the ERP application the parent company has implemented. However, we've observed situations where this application does not support the division's business model and processes well. In cases like this, it makes more sense for the division to choose an ERP system that fits the business and report financial data to the parent organization.

Reporting Requirements

Another level of complexity lies with reporting. In certain cases, and in certain types of businesses, the reporting requirements drive the selection of the ERP application. Unlike earlier systems when accounting applications did not have much of business processes incorporated into them, today's applications come with a lot of business intelligence or data warehouse functionality and have proven to be sufficient for many small and medium-sized organizations. However, in the case of larger organizations which might be a division of a corporate entity and separate from a financial perspective, sometimes the division would have to deal with multi-company, multi-location, or multi-currency requirements; hence the process becomes even more complex, elevating the requirements of the ERP application.

CHAPTER 2 - IMPLEMENTATION COST AND TIMING

For a company with 60 users and $25M in revenue, about how much time and money would be required to implement a replacement ERP application?

To answer this question appropriately, several components of cost must be considered.

It is important to look at all elements of cost when considering an ERP system implementation or migration. Hardware (virtual and physical), software, and services are the most obvious components. However, the less obvious include internal resources, time away from day-to-day operations of the business, and unforeseen impacts on product delivery, customer service, and the collection of receivables.

Hardware and Software

When considering an ERP application for a company with about 60 users and $25 million in revenue, the obvious costs include hardware and software licensing. However, at that size range, the bigger part of bringing in a new solution is going to be the cost of implementation. In general, the cost of implementation will be somewhat higher relative to the cost of the software. At that size range the low end of basic implementation may be $20,000, however, companies may choose to go for much more complex and expensive solutions. The ultimate goals to keep in mind would be to meet multiple needs of the business. Depending on the situation, this may involve bringing in ancillary solutions like EDI, document management, and manufacturing or distribution solutions, and barcode scanning solutions. When all these other complexities are added into an implementation, the cost increases up to a quarter of a million dollars or more in some cases. In the case of a manufacturing organization, other solutions that may need to be brought in include sales tax compliance, field service management, project accounting, and document management solutions. There is a lot that is ancillary to the core of ERP solution, but these applications designed to provide that much more in the way of automation, increased productivity, and enhanced visibility of information for the ownership and leadership teams. At enterprise level or a division of an enterprise level corporation, in many cases, the hardware is a relatively small component of the overall cost and the software is more significant. As a rule of the thumb, the cost is in the range of $4,000 to $5,000 per user to purchase the license for the software at the outset. At $5,000 per user, the software cost for 60 users would be about $300,000. Another cost that is somewhat less easy to estimate is the cost of implementation services.

Implementation Services

Generally, organizations that purchase an ERP application will most likely not to try to implement on their own. They will most likely need to engage the services of a consulting firm that is well-versed in the application they are implementing. The service provider will then undertake the process of planning, implementation, and support. To get all these done, the cost sometimes could be same as or up to twice the cost of the software. For example, if the software licenses cost $300,000, the services might be about that much, or perhaps 1.5 times that, or at the extreme, 4 times that amount. The overall cost of hardware, software and services could be about $600,000 to $750,000 and sometimes approaching a million dollars in larger organizations.

These ratios of software cost to services are somewhat "old school" though. In today's modern 'cloud' world they may not directly applicable. For example, a small company might migrate to a new cloud based solution and perhaps they're paying $100-$300 per user per month and have say 10 users. In this scenario that old idea of a ratio between license cost and services is not really applicable. In order to migrate data, tailor the new system to the firm's business process and do some element of training you might be looking at somewhere between $10,000-$100,000 in services depending on the nature of the organization and the complexity of their requirements. Some people as why is there such a big range. It really comes down to time. We'll talk about SaaS solutions and time to implement shortly.

However, it is important to note that the cost of implementing an ERP application for a manufacturing company is always higher than for a distribution company. For instance, if a small manufacturing company is going to expend about a $100,000 to get a new system in place, it is not uncommon for the cost for a logistics company to be $75,000 to $80,000.

Cost of Internal Resources

The cost of internal revenue required for implementing a new ERP application may be a little difficult to quantify. Lots of I/T resources get consumed in the process and everyone who is going to be involved in the implementation of the application will also need to be involved. For example, subject matter experts from Operations, Finance, Inventory Control, Sales, and Purchasing will be needed to support the implementation.

Time to Implement

Some organizations expect their new ERP system to be installed and running in 3 weeks, others 3 months, but that is rarely attainable. Three months might be enough to get some of the planning done before getting started with the implementation. In a situation where there is no system already in place, it may be possible to get something up and running in about 3 months. However, if the company has an existing ERP application and existing processes, all of which are fairly well-tuned, the implementation time could be easily twice or triple that. It is important for companies to realize how much elapsed time and how much effort from their internal resources are going to be required.

To some degree, the timing and cost is dependent on the organization, and how much effort they are willing to put in. For organizations who want to do it themselves, or who are willing to take up a vast majority of the implementation, the cost of implementation goes down significantly. However, the flipside is that the client may not always have personnel that can be dedicated 100% to the project. This is because organizations do not have team members in the wings waiting to tackle a project like this. The personnel in the company who can undertake this, whether in the Sales, Operations, or the Finance departments of the company have other jobs to do; they cannot be totally dedicated to this project. The best they can do is to put some part-time effort into the project, and that is not enough for the kind of tasks involved. If a company can only invest 10% of its human resources into the implementation, then that is going to significantly limit the ability of the service provider to get on with the project, much less deliver on time. There are a lot of things that the service providers can do, but there are still things that the client has to be responsible for in any implementation. It is a team effort and in order to get the job done, the service provider requires the client's interaction. In general, the adoption of an ERP application by the team members who are going to operate it is always advisable. If for any reason, they are so stuck to the existing process or they are unfamiliar with the new one, or training was insufficient, the implementation takes longer and costs more money. Oftentimes, the fault lies not with the software provider or the consulting firm, but the organization's internal personnel.

Change Management

The change management aspects of bringing in a new ERP solution or any other business solution is a critical element for the organization to understand. If the users are unwilling to change, and if the senior management is not engaged in ensuring the change process is successful, then the project is going to be very difficult. If the users fail to embrace the training or if they don't take advantage of it and commit themselves into learning the new solution, it doesn't matter how much time the consulting firm or software provider invests in the project, the job will still be difficult to execute to completion. The inability or unwillingness of the users to learn and adjust to the new system typically means that the consultants must start teaching the process afresh and this would delay the go-live process.

Software as a Service (SaaS)

Many clients have questions about software as a service (SaaS) solutions, their cost, and time to implement. The truth about it is that many vendors of software publishers are out there trying to get clients to buy their software. In some cases, clients spend hundreds of thousands of dollars on software licensing. As you might guess, this this becomes a deterrent to many organizations. Vendors seems to have universally evaluated this and come up with a SaaS or SaaS like solution. SaaS solutions are typically sold on monthly subscription basis. Hence, instead of spending something like $300,000 on software licensing, subscribers only have to pay about $300 per user per month per user. This presents a great opportunity for the vendors to attract lots of clients, but the burden then lies in the cost of implementation.

NetSuite and Microsoft Dynamics 365 are examples of applications that are considered to be SaaS, and many other applications are following the same path. From a financial perspective, the consultant can make the upfront cost for the client relatively modest for services since the hardware and software have already been provided by another party for a monthly fee.

From a standpoint of functionality, the critical factor is not whether it is software as a service or it is hosted some place in the cloud. What does matter is the systems functionality and how well it fits into the business processes.

There are clients with in-house servers, in the past three years especially, who have heard a lot about the cloud and want to go to the cloud. They want software as a service cloud based solution, and if they find a product that is fit for them, that would be perfect. However, the challenge with the software as a service licensing model is that it doesn't change the amount of time it takes for the solution to be implemented. So, essentially only the cost structure for acquiring the license has been changed into a monthly cost, but the complexity of the solution and the amount of time required for implementation has not changed. The significant thing is that the service has been moved to a cloud-based solution and there will no longer be any need to install the software on a physical server. However, that is just a small fraction when compared to the time it takes for the overall implementation of a solution. This is one of the challenges for many mid-market customers, as they don't understand that though the cost structure has changed, the time required for an implementation and going live has not been eliminated. This is a piece of information the vendors do not tell customers as they go around telling them how easy it is to embrace their applications. The truth is, despite the change in payment structure, the service requirement doesn't change; some number of hours are still needed from the service provider and from the internal personnel within the organization.

CHAPTER 3 - DATA MIGRATION

What does a data migration from an old to a new ERP application entail?

There are several considerations and, if this is not done correctly, the implementation process becomes much more difficult.

Data migration involves taking the data from an old ERP application to the new. It is very important to apply adequate resources to the migration of data from the old to the new ERP application. Further, it is critical to validate this data migrated accurately during the pilot test phase. Going into production with faulty or incomplete data can create a daunting situation for the entire organization.

Responsibility for the Integrity of data

Ultimately, clients are responsible for the integrity of the data. They have to be able to own their data and understand it so well that that they can guide I/T personnel when they are not putting the data in the right places. Clients also need to be involved in terms of answering vital questions, such as when loading phone numbers. For example, the client needs to explain that everybody used dashes or if some people used asterisks or periods in a phone number. If these irregularities are not handled properly it could become a giant problem in the data migration. Inconsistent use of the prior system is another challenge which will necessitate a cleanup in the data migration process.

Some of the newer applications have some intelligence built into them. For example, when the data migration of a phone number comes across, it can detect irregularities so that they can be corrected without separate data cleanup task. One tactic that may be appropriate is to load summary data without the corresponding detail. This commonly occurs with GL data. which has a large number of component transactions. What companies sometimes do is carry the summary data at the GL summary level, including the balance for each account by month and move them over to the new ERP application rather than trying to load in all the underlying detail. This is helpful if the value of the detail data is in question. This requires that the client's accounting personnel do a monthly, quarterly, or year-end comparison on a transaction basis, which doesn't make a lot of sense.

Which Data to Migrate

The data migration can be classified into different segments; the static master data being the simplest of them all. This includes the bills of material, routings, data that pertain to customers and vendors. The second includes open data; open sales orders, open purchase orders, open production orders and the like which are easy to migrate. Historical data such as transaction by transaction sales history and similar information that goes back in time pose a great challenge during the migration process.

Where possible, instead of migrating historical data, consultants try to encourage clients to look at an archive or a data warehouse solution. For the data that are transactional in nature, having access to the old system for a period of time and having access to a data warehouse with the transactional data in It often turns out to be a better solution that migrating historical transactions into the new ERP application. Training users in a newly migrated company on sales orders and purchase orders is generally a straightforward task.

Length of Time Historical Data Need to be Maintained

It is relatively rare to lose access to historical data. However, if that is the case, it is perfectly normal and reasonable to move the data into the data warehouse. But the other realization is that, to some degree, that data is not going to be important in a year or two years' time. By that time, that data is going to be very useless. There aren't too many organizations, especially small and mid-market companies who do look back and do financial analysis going back more than 12 to 24 months. Most of these companies are growing so quickly that what they did 3 to 5 years ago isn't very relevant to the way they are running their business today. So, in most cases, there is not much value in bringing over all the historical data.

Generally, for most clients, 12 months of historical data is enough to migrate and do a year-over-year review, a month-to-month comparison, and similar analyses which is inexpensive from a data migration standpoint.

The Overall Cost of Data Migration

The cost of data migration depends mainly on the type of data to be migrated and then what tools are used in the migration process. These factors determine migration cost even within QuickBooks. For instance, a client once wanted to migrate data from a QuickBooks Online solution. She wanted to migrate all of the data to a new solution, including the line item details within the general ledger. Most, if not all of the solutions on the market today do not have a migration tool that can get to that level of transaction detail and migrating that entails taking monthly or quarterly snapshots of the company's financials. However, this client wanted all the transaction details migrated over to the new solution. So, when the service providers discussed the requirement with the software vendor and gave the client a quote of about $10,000, the client said it was expensive and decided to go on a personal search for a cheaper solution. She went online and got someone who said he could do it at $ 5,000, half of the price the first consultant quoted. The vendor began the project for the client and, within a relatively short period of time, the original estimate of the effort went out of the window. The client had already spent, at that point in time, the original $5,000 and the vendor kept coming back to demand more money until the client ended up spending about $20,000 for the data migration.

The client ended up spending two times of what she was originally quoted by the consultants. It was a no-win situation for the consultants because they could not their client, "I told you so." even though they really wanted to.

The company ultimately did go live, but the amount of time it took them to get through that was almost twice the time initially estimated. From that standpoint, it was much delayed and obviously, the cost of the overall project was quite a bit larger than expected. This made the client very unhappy. That is a kind of worst case scenario of how things can go badly in data migration project. When things go great, everybody just looks at it and says that it is simple, but to be realistic, it is never simple.

The Costs of an Incorrect or Incomplete Data Migration

In another client situation, the data migration project had been done poorly. What was perceived to be a training issue was actually a data migration problem. The sales orders that were supposed to be open and have historical information were transferred haphazardly. As a result, the users were not able to get their sales orders out, couldn't get their invoicing done, couldn't get their cash collected, and ultimately had some financial difficulty as a result of those delays. The consultants were willing to help them get through those difficulties, but their solution was to go back to their original provider and ask for the additional time or free consulting get through their challenges. Financially, the client suffered a great deal before they got things straightened out. Data migration has, on the surface, a very straightforward nature, however, if not done properly, it could have some serious financial implications.

Migration Tools

Migration from QuickBooks is probably the most commonly used solution for small businesses. Many vendors on of ERP software have created tools to enable the migration of some of that data to the new solution making the process relatively easy. In many situations, ERP applications have data import tools to provide a way to utilize data from various sources, including Excel spreadsheets.

Data Cleanup Prior to or During Migration

One thing clients often fail to take note of is that there is a data cleanup task that needs to be completed, and it has to be done by them. Service providers and consultants may extract data and normalize the data for the new system, but that's just data. They just look at it and make sure that things appear the way they should. They ensure that for instance, an address looks like an address, a phone number like a phone number, and a zip code like a zip code, etc. The consultants look at those things and make sure that they appear as they should, but if the client has for instance, an item number in an item description field, or if the client uses another field within the system for something else completely, the consultants may not take notice of that.

Benefits of a Data Warehouse in Data Migration

Our consultants once helped a client get off a legacy application on to something that was well accepted by corporate and the process was turned out to be straightforward. There was no need to do a bunch of data migration work because the client already had a data warehouse solution that was provided to them by the consultants years prior. Hence, the process of using the data warehouse to complete the migration to the new ERP application was relatively simple.

CHAPTER 4 – ACTIVITIES DURING AN IMPLEMENTATION

What activities should clients expect during an ERP system implementation?

There are many activities, internal and external to the organization that need to be addressed.

These activities need to be identified, documented, and executed in the process of implementation. A planning document with milestones is useful to define what needs to be accomplished at keeps the project team on track. In general, organization perform well by completing one milestone before moving on to the next.

Activity 1: Conduct a Discovery in the Office

The first phase of most projects is to explore some elements of a deeper-dive discovery process in the client's organization. Consultants get in, under the covers, to review the organization's internal business processes, and begin to map out what will be the new ERP solution. To do this, the consultant must interact with both the senior executive team and the key personnel who are responsible for critical points in various business processes within the organization. For instance, in a manufacturing organization, an implementation would require an interaction with Controller and Chief Financial Officer along with key personnel in Operations and Sales.

Activity 2: Conduct A Discovery on the Shop Floor

The next phase is to look at the key personnel from the side of the organization's warehouse and manufacturing operations and people who take responsibility for the distribution, sales and marketing, to identify what their information requirements are. In many cases, people in sales and marketing department will need information from production at the end of the day. For example, they need to know when they can sell, from where they can sell it, and how long products will be in production before they are available for sale. These requirements important to define an overall solution. The important part from the consulting side is to understand all the complexities in the client's business processes.

Activity 3: Planning Document with Milestones

Typically, the implementation process has milestones like:

Milestone	Related Activity
Business Process Analysis	Reviewing and documenting the organization's business processes
Project Planning	Identifying the tasks necessary to complete the project and assigning responsibility and timeframes to complete
Software Development / Enhancement	Modifying or customizing the system to accommodate specialized business processes or increase user adoption
Unit Testing	Testing by the software developers to verify that the software enhancements meet the technical specifications
User Acceptance Testing	Testing by the users of the system to validate that the

	software enhancements meet the requirements of the project
Pilot Test 1 (with manually keyed data)	Testing all aspects of the new system of using a manually keyed data
Pilot Test 2 (with migrated data)	Testing all aspects of the new system using data migrated from the old system
Training	Training of the end users by key project team members
Documentation	Document business processes, high-level, and detailed "desk" procedures
Go Live	Transition from the old to the new ERP system

Post-Implementation Support	Address any issues that arise after the new system has been implemented

These should be included in a planning document with start dates, due dates, responsibility, and status. Tools like Microsoft Projects are very helpful in developing an implementation plan, however, in many cases, a detailed Excel spreadsheet will suffice.

Activity 4: Documentation of Existing Business Process

Developing a roadmap for the implementation has some similarities to planning software development. Drawing certain aspects from lean programming methodology and incorporating them into the implementation of has some distinct benefits. For example, the discovery process enables the project team to look at the business as a whole and gives it a chance to critically evaluate and document specific business processes. From there, the team can begin the process of mapping the data points, defining the work flow, and that fitting the business processes into the functionality of the new solution.

Activity 5: Assess Whether Business Processes Fit with System Functionality

It is critical to make some assessment regarding how well the business processes fit with the ERP application. At this point, the team has the chance to develop a plan for execution, akin to a specifications document in software development. The plan may include getting inefficient business processes rolled out so that the project team can see how the new system can be used to make them more efficient.

Activity 6: Reengineer the Business Processes

In the beginning of an implementation project, the process may include reengineering the workarounds that were implemented because of the limitations of current system. Instead of forcing the old processes into the new system, there is an opportunity for the consulting team to explore those processes with the client and potentially to reengineer them to take advantage of the new system or a newer way of completing the work. It may involve some other technology as well. For example, in a distribution or a manufacturing environment, the team might consider bringing in barcode scanning application as a part of the project. This can radically change some of the requirements for inventory management. Business process reengineering is an important part of the overall solution implementation. Once done, the newly defined processes must be tested to validate that they are going to be more efficient than the existing processes. These are all critical tasks for the customer, and cannot be done in absentia with the consultants working independently without coordinating with the project team.

Activity 7: Allocate All Needed Resources

This is a team project. Resources from the client's and from the consulting firm must work together very tightly as an integrated unit. This is needed to ultimately bring a complete solution, that is going to meet the needs of the organization, to fruition. In other words, at the final go-live phase, there is a smooth transition to from the old to the new ERP solution.

Activity 8: Create Documentation

Documentation falls into two broad categories. One is related to the business processes. These include swim lanes and flow diagrams that document how processes are supposed to be executed. It also includes how system processes should be mapped into the business process. The other category is procedural documentation. This is often written at a high level. However, sometimes, there is also a need for some detailed "desk" procedures that describe specific steps for team members to process transactions in the new system.

In both categories, documentation is important to the client. In the first one, which involves mapping out the business processes, documenting those processes also a part of the step of validating them with customers. Members of consulting team must map them out, as they understand them from the client's perspective. In this way, the consulting team can reproduce the business processes in written form so that the customer can review and validate them. This a key step before the project team infuses the business processes into the workflow of the new system. It is critical for customers to look at what has been done, and indicate whether things are done correctly, and communicate whether a step was missed. It is necessary for the consultants to understand all the details correctly and the optimal way to understand them is to document them.

Activity 9: Train End-Users

There is a for need understanding and skillfulness on the part of the end users of the new system. This can be obtained through reading training guides, handbooks, or system documentation. Some organizations choose to train their personnel, but some do not. This kind of investment, in fact, can pay off with big dividends for organizations in the long run. The potential downside of not training manifests itself when a key member of the project team leaves the organization during the implementation or shortly afterwards. This is compounded if she does not transfer the knowledge to her successor. When the successor takes up the role of the departing team member, but does not know what his basic job is nor how to execute it, a retraining process must be undertaken at that point. This retraining process increases the cost of implementation in most cases. However, having a training guide or procedural documentation on hand can alleviate some of the stress and unnecessary expense because there will be a smoother succession if there is some baseline transfer of knowledge.

CHAPTER 5 - COMMON ISSUES DURING IMPLEMENTATION

What kinds of issues commonly arise during an ERP system implementation?

The variety of issues that could arise is pretty broad. They range from data migration problems to overlooked "shadow" business processes to user adoption. If these can be identified and planned for in the analysis stage, the implementation will go much more smoothly.

Issue 1: The Scope of the Project Changes Significantly

Change in the scope of the project is most likely going to be the most significant issue. It comes because of exposure to the capabilities in the new system.

It is like bringing in a piece of new technology that has a thousand bells and whistles to it. However, organization was only expecting to deploy maybe a hundred of those bells and whistles.

Then as the customer becomes more exposed to the capabilities of the system they may see something in there that they like. It wasn't part of the initial requirements. It wasn't part of the wish list per-se. It's something that they didn't even know could be part of the solution, but now they see it in the system and they want it.

It's like when you go new car shopping and you are suddenly exposed to a backup camera on a new car. If you've never had a backup camera before you don't think that it's really that much of a requirement. Because you've driven for 20 years without a backup camera before and you've never had an accident, you may ask if you really need one of those? You get in the car the first time and you put the car in reverse and all of a sudden, you see the backup camera. Perhaps, it's a life-changing moment when you realize, "Wow, I really love this technology. I love the fact that I can see what's going on behind me. I want and need that now."

Something akin to this often happens during the implementation. When a new requirement pops up from nowhere, there becomes a question for the organization, "What do we do? Do we implement this now or wait for Phase 2?"

Issue 2: The Cost and Timing Estimates Were Too Optimistic

When there is a new project, there is usually a budget allocated to it. So, the question becomes, "Can we fit this new item into the original budget?" In some cases, it is possible, while in other cases, it is not. In such situations, the project team has to make a decision to either remove something else from the scope in order to fit in the new requirement or to add extra resources in the form of money and time to the project. It is a decision that the project and executive teams within the customer's organization must make together.

Issue 3: The Impact on Internal Personnel Was Larger Than Expected

While the consulting team can certainly help, internal resources, especially from subject matter experts are critical to the success of the implementation. 25% - 30% is probably a good estimate of the amount of time required to complete the project in a timely fashion. Staff turnover is certainly a situation where issues are likely to arise during implementation.

Issue 4: Unforeseen Gaps Between Business Processes and System Functionality

In many cases business processes and functions were put in place based on the prior system or the prior process, even if it was a paper-based process. There were some rules and some boundaries put in place about the way things were supposed to be done. When bringing in a new piece of technology for the organization, gaps are bound to exist between the business processes and the system's functionality.

Issue 5: Inadequate Processes to Manage Change within the Organization

Change management is the discipline that defines how companies prepare and support team members to successfully adopt change and create organizational success. Managing change in a company is one of the biggest challenges that arises during an implementation. In general, how well the organization manages change is a critical success factor in such projects.

Issue 6: Biting Off More Than the Organization Can Handle

Biting off more than the organization can handle, in this context, refers to "over-implementation" or overreaching during an implementation. In general, if it is possible, the way to avoid this is to take on an initial phase, get that squared away and then take on a Phase 2. Sometimes things go a little bit better than trying to complete the work in Phases 1 and 2 in one shot. A phased implementation sometimes works better, especially if the organization doesn't have spare human resources internally. If the number of people that can apply themselves to completing an implementation is relatively small, it's often better to do things in small chunks as opposed to large. From a cost-benefit perspective, organizations can derive the benefits of the Phase 1 functionality, while working of Phase 2.

Issue 7: Incomplete or Incorrect Data Migration

As stated earlier, there are situations where the data migration is not up to specification or the data migration process is not completed on time. This situation often arises when you try to complete tasks in parallel with the hope that they dovetail at the right time for a pilot test. Sometimes the timing doesn't quite work out, or maybe the migration team does finish what it thinks is correct, but when it finally comes down to testing, data entry and reporting processes just fail. The sales orders won't ship, you can't get the invoices out, and you can't collect cash all because data migration was done incorrectly.

Issue 8: Including Accounting at the End of the Implementation

Finance is often the last functional area to get a handle on what's happening in the system, and unfortunately or fortunately all roads lead to Finance. At the end of the day, within most organizations things boil down to either time or money and that's the purview of the Controller and the CFO. How those resources, whether it's time or money are allocated is driven back to them. Although they don't necessarily hold primary responsibility for the allocation of those resources, they do seem to hold responsibility for the reporting the use of those resources in many cases.

In general, the difficulties for Finance come from the manufacturing end of the ERP application. All the sales orders, purchase orders, accounts receivable, and accounts payable, kinds of things fold into the general ledger well. However, when it comes down to inventory control, movement of inventory from place to place, issues of inventory into production orders, and then receipts into finished goods, the flow of data becomes less clear. The calculations of purchasing and manufacturing variances become the bane of Accounting and no one really understands them, except for Accounting. One of the interesting things we've unserved is that a many team members within the organization don't understand the complete process. Exceptions are typically found in the Finance organization where some personnel actually have a good perspective on what that overall process really does look like from point to point within the organization.

CHAPTER 6 – ENGAGING A CONSULTING FIRM FOR IMPLEMENTATION

Why should firms consider engaging a consulting firm to assist during an ERP system implementation?

It often comes down to not having enough available internal human resources.

Without some level of consulting support, it is very difficult to learn the application, execute the implementation tasks, and manage day-to-day activities all at the same time. Also, there is often justification to temporarily engage additional staff-level resources to support day-to-day activities while the implementation is under way.

Reasons to Do It Yourself

If you have the resources and the knowledge to implement the solution entirely by yourself, then you don't need a consulting organization. However, we have encountered literally one scenario where a client implemented its ERP system completely by itself. It was a function of the COO of the organization, a brilliant guy, who had graduated from UCLA with a master's degree in computer science. More importantly, he was the son of one of the owners and they spent the time to implement the solution. It took about 6 to 9 months elapsed time to implement the solution. To put that into perspective, with a consulting organization helping, an implementation of that nature would typically be completed in 3 to 4 months.

If there is sufficient knowledge within the organization to implement on its own, then that it is reasonable to go ahead and try that. In another case a prospective client, a relatively small service organization, with one person in the finance area, decided to go it alone. She is contemplating implementing an ERP application although just the accounting portion into the organization. She has worked with this package before and she understands the chart of accounts structure very well. She can basically do all the work herself, perhaps with a little of help here and there more on the technical side. Conceptually she could do the entire thing herself without much consulting help at all.

At the other end of the spectrum, some clients that are large, enterprise-sized, organizations can implement on their own. In one case, a client has an I/T staff of 35, which is the size of some small businesses. The team members have quite a lot of experience in supported ERP applications and can essentially implement on their own.

In a final case, the client was a division of a larger parent organization. The parent organization has a similar situation, where they have I/T people on staff, all well-versed in the same ERP application. As divisions come up on this application the corporate office can send out teams of people to get these implementations going and they need very little help from the outside in terms of consulting and resources. The consulting engagement for this particular client was basically to get some data off of the legacy application in a format that could be imported in the new system. After that, corporate resources completed the rest of the work. It was amazing.

Reason 1: Time to Implementation

In the first example, above, it took about twice as much of the organization time to implement that solution. It was, however, a choice that the client made.

Let's use an analogy, a couple retired several years ago, and decided to go and build a house on their own. They had inherited some land and they wanted to build a house on the land. The husband was retiring and had some prior experience and background in the construction industry. So, he had some knowledge but he'd never done anything like this before. He thought it'd be a fun hobby. They went ahead and started the process of constructing their home. They originally estimated that it would take them about a year to build the home. They began the process and they were living in a little mobile home type of place on the property while they were going through the construction.

They had the time, they had the resources, and they also felt that doing it themselves would save them a bunch of money. That was their perspective going into it. In the end, their original estimate of the time to complete of one year was closer to five years. When they finally got the house finished, cost of the overall construction was two times what it had originally been estimated. The couple, in the process of building, realized they didn't have all the knowledge that they needed and ended up bringing in some contractors along the way to do parts of the construction. So, in the end, their cost ended up being 2x of their original budget for the project and their time investment was almost 5x of their original estimate. This is the kind of challenge that exists in ERP systems implementations.

Client Responsibilities	Service Provider Responsibilities	Resulting Action Item
Provide access to subject matter experts (SMEs), usually key managers and supervisors	Gather available documentation and requirements for the new ERP system	Discovery document and implementation plan
Define and document existing business processes	Review existing businesses process and identify gaps	Map existing business processes into functionality of the new ERP system
Identify and document key business requirements of the ERP new system	Review requirements and identify any missing components	Identify possible sources of missing functionality, including 3rd party applications and

		custom software development
Provide access to the existing system and related data	Review existing data structures and content	Map data from the old into the new ERP system
Testing: User acceptance and pilot testing	Unit testing of various software components, coordinate user acceptance and pilot testing	Identify and address any gaps in functionality or new requirements
Training: Allocate key personnel who will be in training and designated to train others in their functional areas	Provide training to key personnel in all functional areas impacted by the new system	Create high level procedural documentation
Documentation: Provide detailed	If needed, developed desk	Validate documentation

procedural documentation for all personnel responsible for the transition from table to the new ERP system	procedures for personnel responsible for data entry	with results of pilot tests
Go live: Allocate all necessary resources to transition from the old to the new ERP system	Observe operation of the new system to ensure that it is working as expected	Identify and, as quickly as possible, addressing the issues that arise after going live

Reason 2: Overall Cost of Implementation

You can do it yourself, but you may find that, in fact, you don't save any money and you certainly don't do it any faster, and that's the challenge. You are not gaining the benefits of the solution that you've selected as quickly as you need to. Part of the calculation of bringing in a new solution is that return on the investment. In other words, "How quickly can I achieve a return on the investment that I'm making or bringing in new technology." Regardless of what that technology is, whether it's ERP or CRM or whatever it might be, part of it is a simple return on investment (ROI) calculation. The longer it takes to attain that ROI the less valuable it is to the organization. In part, that's just driven by the time/value of money. In other words, the value of a dollar today is actually higher than the value of a dollar three years from now. Hiring a consultant helps you reduce the cost of implementation and reap the benefits sooner.

Reason 3: Insufficient Internal Human Resources

Having knowledge and experience is essential, but the challenge is that is in most organizations, you have people who already have full-time jobs. They are a controller, an accountant, a manufacturing person or a warehouse manager. Whatever their job function may be they have a full-time job already. The company is paying them a salary and potentially some additional compensation above and beyond that, but they already have a full-time job. How much additional time do they have to put towards the implementation of new technology? Maybe that's 10%; maybe that's 20%. In many cases, that's about as much as is obtainable in most organizations. These people already have full-time jobs and they could potentially put in 45 or 50 hours in a week. Maybe they could dedicate five to ten of those hours towards the implementation of a new solution. That's about it. So, that determines how quickly companies can embrace the new solution and how quickly they can bring that return to the organization and get started with that goal and realizing the benefits of it.

CHAPTER 7 - MANAGING THE DATA IN THE OLD SYSTEM

What have clients typically done with the data in the systems they are migrating from?

Regarding the data in the previous system, there are a few decisions to make. Often the approach will depend on the organization's assessment of future requirements.

The issue of what to do with data from the previous system has a few facets. Often the answer depends on:

- What the client expects to use this data for

- How long it needs to be available

- the budget available to put a solution in place

For example, if the data is only required for reporting purposes, a data warehouse might be best. If there are regulatory requirements (e.g., FDA, HIPPA, etc.), a working read-only version of the old system might be the most sensible solution. In the discussion that follows, we'll touch on these tradeoffs and present solutions for a few of these situations.

Maintain the Old System

The old system still matters to some extent. Flipping the switch and moving everybody over to the new system does not make the old system to automatically vaporize. In most cases, it is still going to continue operating in one form or another. If for instance, we are talking about a QuickBooks system, it is probably on someone's desktop somewhere. If the data is there and if they need to do a look back for some reason, they can certainly do that. The flipside to this is that the value of that data diminishes over time. It's not like wine. It doesn't get better with age. So, from the standpoint of usability, in the first few months of the new system being live, the data in the old system will be of some value. However, it wouldn't be cost-effective for the consulting team to invest a ton of time and of effort because a client uses something like this. Over time, say a year or two later, the data is probably not going to have a whole lot of value to it.

Data Warehouse

There may be legacy transactional data that is not to be migrated over and if the desire is to have access to that in the future, then one option that can be done is to migrate that data into a data warehouse. A data warehouse is simply a database that stores information from the old system a user-friendly format. This serves two purposes: 1) storage of the historical information and 2) a valuable tool for reporting.

Timeframes

Typically, a one or two year's timeframe is involved. There was a client who went off the old system in February of and as the year rolled on, there were another two or three requests for some reporting. From that point, demand was expected to diminish fairly quickly over the following years. In that particular case, the data reporting that was generated from the data warehouse, not necessarily from the system itself. HIPAA probably has the longest retention requirements, up to seven years. In situations like that, clients will shut down the system and keep everything intact (if they have space). Then, if they have requirement, I/T would bring the system back up again to allow users to access the data for reporting as necessary. However, this is a rare situation. It isn't that common for users to need to go back to the old system five years after it was shut down.

Regulatory Requirements

When there is some kind of necessity from a regulatory standpoint, for example in the healthcare industry, organizations do need to keep data, depending upon the nature of the data, for up to 10 years. So, there are some scenarios where from a regulatory standpoint, they do need to keep their data and that's the scenario where we would look at a data warehouse. Otherwise, for most clients, the old system isn't just going to go away overnight when they begin using the new system. From a transactional standpoint, it's still there. It's an archive at that point and, if company needs to go back into it, they certainly can.

Platforms

When it comes to the regulatory side, FDA requirements for pharmaceutical companies or food and beverage manufacturers are for 10 years. This applies to record keeping on manufactured parts as they must keep track of all the manufacturing of all the components used down to the raw material level, with traceability for all those items. Again, most clients don't operate in a stringent regulatory environment, so they don't have the need to hang on to the historical data archive as much. However, when they do, then the data warehouse absolutely makes sense for them.

In some cases, it makes sense to keep the old system running for a period of time, maybe 1 or 2 years, where it's up and online all the time. After that point, the utilization of that system typically diminishes quickly. The one exception to that would be maybe if it's something that's on an old platform. We migrated some clients from a UNIX platform onto something that was more current (i.e., a Windows platform), usually running a different ERP package. What happens to the old system? It's a little bit tough sometimes to keep a UNIX system running for very long especially if the hardware is somewhat old. In situations where that system was migrated to Windows platform and then migrated off to another ERP application, then maybe it's not quite as difficult because clients can typically operate the Windows platform for quite a long time. In the migration process, we usually end up getting some number of data files off the old system to do the migration to the new system. But oftentimes, it's not the full set of data that should be looked at. Some data that should be included are master data and open transactions, like open sales, purchase orders, and production orders. However, the historical information about the sales orders, purchase orders, and work orders are typically not carried across to the new system. They usually end up in the legacy system or in the data warehouse for future review.

Older Methodologies

Older methodologies include reel to reel tapes and more recently jukeboxes of tape cartridges for backup. One of the problems these storage methodologies is that in order to be able to use those tapes, clients must have a system that is roughly the same as the equipment that created them. Sometimes, it's not so easy to reproduce that system even if you have those tapes.

That creates a different set of challenges. On the other side of that, some clients who had all of those records, at least with respect to any manufacturing records being kept on paper, would have to archive 10 years' worth of paper documents. The storage requirements on that alone were onerous. So, the move to electronic documentation for clients like that can ultimately saving them a lot of time, money, and effort.

CHAPTER 8 - CUSTOM SOFTWARE DEVELOPMENT

Under what conditions should an organization pursue custom software development?

While custom software development helps to fit the ERP application to existing business processes, there are cost / benefit tradeoffs to consider.

Custom software development can be a valuable tool in getting an ERP system into place. It helps to make the software better fit the organization's business processes. The primary downside is that the custom software enhancements need to reviewed and, in some cases, redone when the underlying software is upgraded to the most recent version. A potentially worse outcome is that custom software development is used to streamline an inefficient business process. In the discussion that follows, we'll discuss a few of the tradeoffs.

The 80 / 20 Rule

The 80 / 20 rule applies to ERP system implementations. Organizations should aim to get 80% of the functionality that it needs "out of the box". In other words, get 80% of the required functionality without making any system modifications. For some clients, 80% was really all they needed. They may be able to get 100%, however, in some cases, there are unique challenges or unique needs within the organization. So, it becomes necessary to look for an out of the box software package. The implementation team would typically aim to accomplish about 80% of the requirements in an out of the box solution. It would then look at what to customize and keep that fairly limited (tight in scope) to address the remaining 20% of the equation. The goal is to meet the specific needs of the organization; however, it has to be with respect to the way that the business processes should be run (rather than how they exist). One of the challenges that exists around software development is when the client requires that the consultants to customize the new solution to effectively work the way the old solution did. This is definitely a difficult situation from a consultant standpoint because, in most cases, ERP systems are built to subscribe to industry best practices.

Specialized Business Processes

If the consultants must deviate from the way the new system is designed to function, there must be a good reason for that. Generally, "It's because that's the way the old system worked." isn't a good enough reason for such a deviation.

It would require changing the business process in those cases and that's the change management side of implementing the new system. That can be one of the most difficult challenges with respect to implementation and acceptance of new technology.

In the late 1990's and early 2000's, the systems that came out for ERP back then might not have always been a good fit for the client. Hence, some number of software development changes, sometimes minor, sometimes major, were required to put some subsystems into place. These were often specific to the client organization. As time has gone passed, the requirements for custom software development have diminished, partly because there are additional pieces of functionality in the software that fit business processes better. So, the software development requirement today is somewhat smaller than it was back then.

Third-Party Applications

The other thing that exists in the marketplace today, for virtually all major ERP solutions, is that most of them have an ecosystem of third-party applications built around them. These augment the core functionality of those systems. We have third party-packages that meet specific unique industry needs whether it's something like credit card processing, equipment rental, barcode scanning, or EDI. There are quite a few products that are out there today that tie into many of these mid-market ERP solutions. These applications meet a specific need that the publisher of the software may not have included in the core functionality of its product. These products are natively integrated into the environment and do not require the custom development that used to be necessary in the past. Now, it is more of a function of finding the correct third-party solution. This alleviates a lot of challenges of related to ERP software upgrades because there is now a third-party software publisher that is managing that product. In other words, the third-party application provider is taking care of the updates and upgrades to the product.

Third-party application providers are maintaining their integration to the main ERP software publisher but whether it's Oracle, Microsoft, Intuit, etc. But the bottom line is they're managing that part of it for the client so it isn't hamstrung by the cost of rebuilding customizations when upgrading to a new version.

Even within the Microsoft ecosystem, this used to be one of the major knocks against products like Microsoft Dynamics GP and AX. Microsoft has spent a lot of time and effort over the past few years to make those upgrades more seamless for customers. Now, while there is Dynamics 365 for operations, what was Dynamics AX or AX7, is a completely cloud and SaaS-based solution.

Dynamics 365 can still be customized, however, there's a customization layer built into it. So, what we see today is the evolution of the software from the publisher side so that, even where there is a case customization, ERP software publishers want customers to be able to upgrade to the latest versions because there are long-term benefits for the publishers in terms of keeping their customers on the latest and greatest version.

When customers fall off that cliff of having a customized solution, what often happens is that those customers choose not to do the upgrades. Further, at some point in time, they choose may choose not to continue to pay the annual software support and maintenance fees. That's a loss for the publishers. So, they've considered ways to try and eliminate that loss. Even in a best case scenario, for some organizations, there will always be a need for some element of customization.

Custom Software Development, Parameters, And APIs

The underlying structure of ERP software has evolved in recent years. In years past, consultants worked directly with the application's source code. Sometimes, they ended up taking a version of source code that was provided by the publisher, made some changes to it, and deployed new versions of the software. Those situations were probably the most difficult for customers from an upgrade perspective.

As time rolled on, many parameters began to creep into the software. Rather than going through the process of making modifications to the software, it just became a matter of changing parameters. Oracle and SAP, for example, have this functionality. Operating the software became a little more complex. Sometimes, it became complex to the point where customers needed to have experts come in as consultants to set those parameters correctly.

One more observable change in this process is the concept of business objects or application program interfaces (APIs). This occurs in SYSPRO and in other applications. SYSPRO does not allow changes to the base functionality of the software. Therefore, the base software always operates as its developers published it. Basically, what third party providers and custom software developers do is write software that communicates to those business objects or APIs. In turn, the business objects will follow well-defined rules to create transactions within the system (e.g., add a sales order, receive cash against accounts receivable, etc.) Since those rules are always followed, the data is always in a consistent within the database.

Custom Software Development and Upgrades

One of the things that poses difficulties for the maintenance of the ERP system is the software upgrade process. As clients upgrade from version to version of the main publisher's software, the custom software development that was done along the way becomes a hindrance. This is because all those customizations must be carried forward into the new version. This effectively increases the cost of the upgrade. In most cases, carrying the upgrades forward is justified and cost-effective for the organization. In other cases, it would be more cost-effective for clients to follow the system's base functionality. This alleviates the need to carry forward the custom software development to subsequent versions.

CHAPTER 9 - USER ADOPTION OF THE NEW ERP SYSTEM

What factors most influence user adoption of a new ERP system?

User adoption is an often overlooked, but key ingredient in ERP systems implementations. Support by I/T and Accounting and smooth transfer of knowledge to the end-users are key factors.

Have you ever experienced or observed situations where a new system implementation was stymied because the users were unable or worse, unwilling, to use the new system? This issue seems to be more common in large organizations where systems functions are defined with some granularity. In the following discussion, we'll present some ideas that may be applicable to your situation.

I/T Support Alone is not Sufficient

If people are on board with the new system coming in and they're excited about it, then user adoption becomes much easier, However, if

1. Users are antagonistic to changing and bringing in new software

2. Team members don't feel like management is engaged in the project

3. This is a scenario where one executive decided to get new software package

4. The implementation of that new solution is largely being driven by IT alone

5. The CEO, the CFO, and other top management staff are not driving the project

then the implementation becomes more challenging because I/T can't drive the project effectively by itself.

I/T needs buy-in from other parts of the organization, depending upon the nature of the organization. If it's a manufacturing organization, then Manufacturing certainly needs to be involved. Finance needs to be involved. The Supply Chain and Operation side of the company needs to be involved. Yes, even the Sales team needs to be involved. If these functional areas are going to be needing information from the system or working with internal information in the way of sales history, purchase orders, and inventory transactions in the system, then they must buy-in early in the process. If they don't, then the organization going to have people who feel that their needs are not be being met and that they're not being listened to in the process. Clearly, that's an internal issue more than a consultant's issue, however, it ends up falling more often than not on the consultants' shoulders. At the end of the day, if the consulting team is tasked with getting the system online and making it work through the organization.

Training and Documentation

Other important factor is the investment in training. Organizations need to make an adequate investment and training and not try to "cheap out" in this area. ERP is the heart and brains while money is the lifeblood of the organization. The ERP system in a business is arguably either the heart or the brain. Either way it's a pretty important organ because the ERP system is keeping the money flowing through the organization regardless of what type of business it is. It is handling all of the financial management for the organization. If we subscribe to the adage that money is the lifeblood of a business then the ERP system is what's driving circulation. It is always amusing when people go into the age of a new ERP system and then try and do it on the cheap because that is generally a failed strategy. When we're looking at something that is this important to the organization in terms of data-driven decision-making and managing the finances of the organization, it is counterintuitive that some organizations try to skimp in places. One of the places that companies oftentimes try to skimp is either in training or documentation. The documentation is often directly tied to training because, in many cases, the documentation they are looking at putting together is training-related. Further, this documentation becomes a post go-live resource for the organization so that executives won't have to call the consultants back because somebody forgot how to perform some function in the system.

Change Management

There is often a need (and it is not always fulfilled) for the users to have some kind of broad knowledge of how the system works as a whole. The policy and procedure documents help to accomplish that. At the most detailed level, there should be a set of desk procedures for team members to follow and as they go through the system. They would know exactly what screens they are supposed to go to and what kind of data should be populated on the fields on that form. That will go a long way to help provide user adoption.

Transfer of Knowledge to the End-Users

As mentioned earlier, getting the new system to work exactly like the old one may not be the best course of action plan, especially if resources (time and money) are limited. However, some customization may be warranted if it can be completed quickly. For example, cosmetic changing the field names to be similar to what was in the old system even though they have different functionality in the new system. So, if a few things occur like that where there is some familiarity between the old and the new systems, the users would adapt more easily to the new package. During the implementation process, there also should be clear division of labor between the consultants and the users in the organization. There have been cases where the consultants were very good at going through the process of getting everything running. They were running all the tests and running all the processes through and trying to make sure that everything flowed properly. Then, at the conclusion of the project, or near the conclusion of the project, the consulting team is withdrawn leaving the system to the users. Unfortunately, when it came to the new system, the users were essentially lost. Without the consultants, the users did not have enough tools to work with the new system and to use it successfully.

Involve Finance and Accounting Throughout the Implementation

It is important to get the Finance and Accounting teams involved early in the implementation process. In many cases, the Accounting and Finance teams don't get involved until late in the system implementation. So, all the operational aspects of the systems are working properly but there wasn't enough thought given to the implications on the general ledger. As transactions flow correctly for shipping and receiving and processing production orders, all of those transactions eventually end up in the general ledger and sometimes the mappings that are set up initially aren't correct. It takes some time to unravel how system transactions were booked to the general ledger and correct the mappings.

Excel Spreadsheets

There was once a client for whom who the consulting team was implementing a new software package. The client had been using an old ACCPAC system for its general ledger. However, Accounting had been tracking all of its costing and manufacturing operations in a series of Excel spreadsheets. The consultants went through the implementation of the new system and as they were getting into the costing of the product that the company manufactured, the client provided the formula it used for its product costing. This formula was entered and tested in the new system.

When it got to the point of validating the system, consultants were going through a user acceptance testing and they started putting some transactions into the system and, at that point, reporting started to come out in the back end. The client got very upset and said that the settings were wrong and that the numbers that were coming out were incorrect. The consulting team went back to the system and determined that they had configured the system in a manner consistent with the formulas and the numbers that the client had provided earlier. They went back to the client and said, "This is what you gave us and this is what we've entered in the system and when we put the transactions through, this is what we get."

What end up happening was the Accounting team had to go back to the product costing spreadsheet and discovered that somebody had changed the formula in the Excel spreadsheet years prior. The subsequent spreadsheets were incorrect and ultimately it became something of a financial disaster for the organization. The Finance team realized this error had added millions of dollars to the bottom line for the product. The client ended up having to go in, because this was a division of a much larger organization, and restate its earnings. Ultimately the CFO was fired and a couple of other people lost their jobs along the way but it turned out that the consultants and the new system were calculating product costs correctly. The new system and the cost numbers that it was generating were correct, however, the old system had been wrong for years and had been actually generating incorrect earning statements for the organization. It was a disaster. Fortunately, the client moved forward and the new system was put in place, but in the process the management team learned the hard way that there are risks associated with managing financial the financial affairs of the company with an unsecured Excel spreadsheet. There's a good justification to get on to an ERP application if the organization has been running much of their business on Excel spreadsheets. With spreadsheets, the risk of having some kind of error, a formula error for example, is very high. There have also been cases where people could not get the spreadsheet to reconcile. So rather than locate the discrepancy, they actually "plugged" the total with a number that tied out to everything else.

CHAPTER 10 - COMMON POST-IMPLEMENTATION ISSUES

After an ERP systems implementation has been completed, what issues should clients be mindful of?

For a period of time, immediately after an ERP systems implementation, it pays to be watchful. Identifying and resolving issues sooner will often be less expensive than doing so later.

Issue 1: Underestimating the scope of the overall project

If you think the system implementation is going to be finished at "go live", you're in for a surprise. In general, after a system goes live there is often work that was planned for in the subsequent phases of the project and, unfortunately, work that wasn't planned for at all. As in many things it is difficult to predict and address every scenario in which something might go wrong. The first few weeks after the ERP system goes live are the most critical.

The thing to be mindful of is that going through go live doesn't mean that that's the end of the consultants' engagement with the system or with the organization. There's always a level of post go-live support that is needed.

In many cases, what we're talking about here is a continuous change element. The initial work up to going live is usually considered to be Phase 1. However, there could potentially be Phases, 2, 3, 4, etc. that could be ongoing within organization from there. There are in many cases the scenarios where the implementation of the new system is just the start of bringing in other elements to help the organization to be more efficient. There's bar code scanning in a distribution or a manufacturing environment and some cases this may not be part of the scope of Phase 1. However, now that the organization has gotten through the initial implementation (e.g., the core financial functionality) of the new system, now the team can start to look at secondary and tertiary elements of the overall implementation.

Issue 2: Not Preparing for Continuous Change Management

For some clients, the implementation creates a cycle that never ends or certainly doesn't end for years to come depending upon where they are and where they are trying go. Change management requires that organizations design a controlled process to identify and implement necessary changes to how work is performed with related adjustments to the ERP application. Clients who use a very low-end accounting systems with just core accounting functions often have everything else being done in spreadsheets. If these clients have visions of going from that to the light speed world of operating like Amazon.com, where everything is digital, they should be cautious and realize that it's not realistic to accomplish this in Phase 1. First off, the timeframe for overall implementation is significant. The change management effort of going through that is tremendous to an organization and the cost in those cases is going to be significant as well. It is important for the consulting team to be realistic with the client.

Clients should expect a multi-phased implementation process that ultimately allows them to accomplish their implementation objectives. However, that may take a year, two years, or three years, depending upon the organization and the requirements that they're trying address. But that's not necessarily a bad thing. It allows executives to budget and manage costs over a multi-year timeframe and, from a financial standpoint, it allows the organization to spread those costs over multiple fiscal years so that it can absorb it over time as well.

Issue 3: Underestimating the Cost of the Overall Project

The other thing to look at is the support side of using the system. How well the users embrace the training in the beginning of the project will determine what the cost of the work on the backend of the implementation is going to be. For example, if during the initial training, people are sitting around, playing with their phones, and coming in and out of the training sessions and not embracing that training opportunity, then when the system goes live, there are going to be challenges. And after going live, there are going to be even more challenges. If the finance team wasn't paying attention, and now this is the first time they're going to have to do a month-end closing on their own on the live system, issues will most likely arise. The consulting team usually goes through the first month-end close with the accounting team. Now it's the second time that they must go through month-end closing and they don't remember how to do it. The consulting team is going to have to help them and hold their hand through that process and that's an extra cost to the organization.

Issue 4: Insufficient Pilot Testing

The adage, "An ounce of prevention is worth a pound of cure" applies. In other words, a little precaution is preferable to a lot of fixing up afterward. An issue that falls into the prevention category is pilot testing. The consultant team should coordinate at least two conference room pilot tests. The basic idea of the first pilot test is to work with some data that was manually keyed in. The objective of the second pilot test is to do some work with some data that has been migrated from the previous application.

In that second pilot test, in theory, users should see all the issues that are going to pop up after going live. It's a critical point in the process of implementation. If users let these issues slip all the way through and "go live", the things they didn't catch in that second pilot test are going to be compounded (in spades) when the system goes into production.

One case in point is the data migration. Data migration ideally should be pristine so that the new system basically has the data from the old system and can operate with it going forward. In one client situation, the data migration was not up to par. The data looked reasonable visually when users reviewed the screens but processing transactions was a different story. For example, the data migration included open sales orders. Customer Service and Inventory Control had so much trouble that they couldn't get product shipped out the door. They had trouble getting shipping paperwork printed, generating invoices, and collecting cash. In this sort of a scenario, not only is it a headache from a change management perspective, it became a serious financial problem as well. It is very important to have as many of these issues as possible squared away during pilot testing before going live.

Issue 5: Not Defining a Fallback Position

One of the issues that also comes to mind is not having fallback a position. If, for some reason, the organization goes live on a new application and there's just a total meltdown on the new system, there must be a way to be able to fall back to a working position. Generally, this means going back onto the old system. It is not always advisable to use double entry to run parallel on both systems for a period of time because that process is just extraordinarily expensive. Users are having a hard enough time dealing with the work that they have on a day-to-day basis. Keeping two ERP systems running at the same time in parallel is a very daunting task. In situations where there is no parallel run before cutting over, there needs to be a fallback position, which is typically to get back onto the old system if things go terribly out of control on the new one.

Issue 6: Not Learning From Earlier Phases to Make the Subsequent Phases Easier

In general, where there is an opportunity to take some small steps, there's a benefit of being able to learn from the earlier phases. That way, the second and third phases can be executed more appropriately. When organizations try to take on Phase 1 through 3 at one time, they almost always end up having some difficulties that they could otherwise have avoided. For example, if an organization were to implement just the financial and logistics portions of the ERP system in Phase 1, then implementing the manufacturing aspects of the system can be approached in a more streamlined manner. In this scenario, the manufacturing module can be configured to meet the accounting requirements which have already been well-defined.

Issue 7: Not Getting a Fast ROI from the Early Phases

Another reason why a multi-phase approach is recommended is that part of what consulting team is trying to do for the organization is get a relatively rapid return on the investment that the organization is making in that new solution. If the implementation of the new system is going to take a year that means it's going to be a year before it can even begin, to recapture any of the investment in the new system. However, if it's possible to implement a subset of the functionality that executives ultimately want to have in Phase 1, then the organization can get a return on that investment fairly quickly. If Phase 1 can be completed in 90 days instead of a year, everybody feels better. The ownership and leadership of the organization feel better at that point because they invested tens of thousands of dollars and see that they are getting some return on that. There's a confidence factor that goes up exponentially when the multi-phased approach is taken. This is a stark contrast to the, "I have to have everything and it all has to be done perfectly and it all has to be done in one phase" approach.

The latter scenario nearly always results in some horrifically bad projects where things really go awry. We caution clients to steer away from that as often as they can because, at the end of the day, it's just not a good scenario for the consulting team or the client. The finger pointing when that starts to happen makes it a bad place for everybody. When going through an implementation like this, these issues have to be discussed in the pilot testing sessions and status meetings. It must be a team approach rather than "you versus me". It's "we" and that's how it is supposed to be. Everybody must work together to be successful. The consulting organization wants its clients to be happy. However, at times, consultants wish that their clients would listen more often than they do.

Clients need to be better off from a financial perspective with the services of the consulting firm than without. If that doesn't happen, then both teams should be looking for another solution. The same can be said about the ERP system. In the early phases of deciding, in system selection phase, there's some justification to figure out what the benefit would be of having the ERP application versus the cost of not having it. From there the executive team can do a little bit of analysis to calculate ROI or net present value (NPV) or whatever makes the most sense for that organization. Once the implementation is done and a period of time goes by (e.g., 6 months), there is a need to take a look at what transpired after the ERP application went live. It's important to know how well it worked and ascertain if organization is going to end up with a positive return on investment.

Issue 8: Not Measuring Overall ROI

The fantasy dream world, from a consulting standpoint, is that the organization estimated the ROI of the project even before starting the implementation of the new system. Also, it would ideal of the executive team had established some goals for what the new solution was going to do for the organization. Then it would be a straightforward process to compare the original estimates of ROI against calculations for six months to a year after going live. Unfortunately, there have been a lot of clients that don't do that type of analysis. Further, they don't review their own internal business process analysis which makes it difficult, for them to do any kind of real estimate of ROI after the fact. Without this data gathering, it is difficult to get a sense of the big picture. In other words, how do clients answer the question, "Was the project profitable overall and to what extent?"

CHAPTER 11 - IoT AND ENTERPRISE RESOURCE PLANNING

What is IoT and how does it apply to enterprise resource planning?

The Internet of Things (IoT) refers to the connection of computer devices embedded in everyday objects. IoT has made its way into manufacturing processes to streamline and make them more efficient.

The Internet of things (IoT) refers to the web-enablement of traditional devices. Increasingly, we see the opportunities for connected devices that were, in the past, stand-alone. To illustrate, a vending machine, typically a stand-alone device, can be equipped with sensors and connected to the Internet. The vending machine can then transmit information about the items sold so that the vending machine operator knows when to come by and refill. The key benefit in this instance is that operator's route can be adjusted to skip the machines that still have items to sell. Using a little math, the vending machine could signal when an item is about to sell out before it actually does!

Home automation is a big deal right now. Sensors installed within the home, can transmit information about temperature, humidity, sound, how movement takes place inside the structure. One of the most common examples is the nest thermostats that we're now seeing available on the market today. Like many things, these can be controlled by a smartphone or other mobile device.

Other examples include things we see every day and the adoption of IoT is growing exponentially. Things like the biometric devices people are carrying and wearing are mobile-enabled, connected to the Internet via wireless networks, and transmitting information to their users.

One of the most common commercial implementations is in lighting in an office building. The lights themselves are equipped with sensors that can sense temperature, humidity, and movement and transmit this information to lighting and HVAC control systems. The result is a savings in the cost of electricity.

There are a lot of benefits that come with IoT and a lot of challenges as well. Data security is the most pressing concern, however, that's a whole other area of the information technology world today.

In manufacturing and other industries, sensing the location and status of inventory, equipment, and personnel may be useful to make them more efficient.

Applications in Manufacturing

In the manufacturing organizations, often there is the equipment on the floor and that the enterprise resource planning application typically doesn't track. For example, the time spent on a particular operation in a production order is recorded, but the number of cycles the machine has been through is not. It is common to see equipment on the factory floor has been enabled with sensors and transmission devices so that its operation can be communicated to a central location. Some of those pieces of equipment have long meantime between failures and can notify maintenance personnel that a power supply or a circuit board needs to be replaced. The sensors can also communicate that a piece of physical machinery is always in use during the manufacturing process. The key advantage in this situation is that preventative maintenance can be scheduled at a convenient time rather than when a failure occurs. Also, the need for periodic maintenance can be reduced in favor of "as needed" predictive maintenance.

Some clients have large pieces of equipment that are deployed to customer locations in the field. Examples include manufacturers of machines that get used for packaging or bottle and can inspection. These machines are almost always complex pieces of equipment of equipment with many components. These pieces of equipment can be equipped with sensors that transmit how they are operating and can communicate to service personnel at the client or customer site, that a component has failed or is about to fail. This affords the opportunity to replace the component before it goes out which reduces or eliminates the downtime that might occur otherwise.

There are also opportunities where clients are producing pieces of equipment that move around. A case in point would be a bus fleet. The operator needs to know something about the pieces of equipment that are driving around on the road, how the equipment is being maintained, and when the next service is required.

Finally, there's an opportunity for application where the organization is in the business of measuring things. For example, measuring the residue that remains on a piece of equipment or component that's going into an aircraft. In those situations, those measuring devices also have the ability to transmit what they're measuring and eliminate a significant portion of the manual data entry. This also eliminates the error that takes place in the recording of that data.

Product Testing

Preventative maintenance is probably the most obvious opportunity for IoT in manufacturing today as there is often an immediate financial benefit to organizations that embrace it. We see this as an area in which there will be even more growth and expansion. Customers today also have much higher demands of consultants and of their suppliers. A client organization provides heat testing and treatment services for the aerospace industry. One of the things that its customers, large aerospace companies, wanted from them was real-time data about the performance or the status of its components. These components were pieces of equipment that were going into giant furnaces. To paint the picture, imagine a very large production facility or huge warehouse-sized furnaces. Literally, a small aircraft would fit into some of these furnaces. Then they would heat treat them, raising them up to temperatures over a thousand degrees and then perform other operations on top of that. The client's customers were looking for them to be able to give them status reports. For example, "Where are my parts in your production process?" They were also looking for the ability for the furnaces to be web-enabled to the point where they could say, "Okay, Mr. Customer, your parts are in furnace number 127 and they're currently at 812 degrees. Oh, now they're at 813 degrees, but still within tolerance." The furnaces had to be web-enabled in order for the client to provide the real-time information its customers were looking for. For a period of time this represented a competitive advantage for the client.

Record-Keeping for ISO Compliance

We've seen quite a few instances where aerospace companies are very stringent about record keeping, especially if there's an ISO 9001 or some other compliance requirement for quality. Those situations require some very good record-keeping about how the testing process went or how that the heat treatment process as described earlier. Those records had to be kept on file for a lengthy period of time, which spanned many years.

In the aerospace industry, the general contractors, like Boeing and Lockheed Martin, were responsible for that record-keeping. Today, much of that has been pushed down to the subcontractors and they're the ones who have to do all of that record-keeping and tracking. That has become a major challenge for those smaller organizations.

CHAPTER 12 - ARTIFICIAL INTELLIGENCE AND ENTERPRISE RESOURCE PLANNING

What is artificial intelligence and how might it apply to enterprise resource planning?

Artificial intelligence, in simplistic terms, is using computer systems to complete tasks that people would normally do. At minimum, artificial intelligence promises to support decision-making and automate certain supply chain functions.

In combination with IoT functionality, artificial intelligence (AI) could well become the "brain" that controls entire manufacturing plants. There is still much work to be done in this area, however, the rate of progress is accelerating. In other words, what took ten years to accomplish ten years ago, will only take a few years today. This will be an exciting area to watch as innovations are brought to market.

Artificial Intelligence and Big Data

Big data refers to extremely large data sets that can be analyzed by computer systems to reveal patterns or trends. IoT is, for better or for worse, a source of lots and lots of data that can hence lead us to questions about big data. Business intelligence tools like Watson Analytics, Microsoft Power BI, and Tableau Desktop can serve to harness these mountains of data. Once the business analytics are in place, the next step in the process is to interpret the data that's coming out of these IoT devices. A related question is, "How can artificial intelligence be applied to enterprise resource planning?" There are many different opportunities to leverage artificial intelligence within the organization, including those that apply to supply chain, inventory control, production, and ordering processes. For example, today, buyers and planners are responsible for keeping inventory at optimal levels. Sales forecasting, Master Production Scheduling (MPS), and Materials Requirements Planning (MRP), guide many organizations' materials management. At some time in the not so distant future, these roles will be replaced by intelligent systems that can keep track of inventory values, determine when inventory will be depleted, and order replacement parts. These parts will arrive just in time to be pulled from their location by a robot or automated conveyor system for the next production order. The next evolution of this paradigm shift is when one organization's AI communicates with other organization's AIs to keep their respective supply chains running smoothly.

Natural Language Processing

We live in a world today where we can choose from Siri, Google Assistant, Alexa, or Cortana and to gain access to an artificial intelligence platform. We can verbally ask for information, have an intelligent agent retrieve it and give it back to us verbally or visually. For example, someone on the shop floor can verbally request the drawings for the part he or she is working on at the time. Tremendous amounts of human and financial resources are being expended in this area by IBM, Google, Amazon, and Facebook. It's going to be an interesting journey. Microsoft is certainly moving in this direction. Cortana Analytics integration is one of the newest features offered in its ERP solutions. We expect this to continue to evolve as new, more powerful computing becomes available and new versions of software are released.

Balance Inventory Carrying Cost and Product Availability

Given a source of historical data, there are ways to predict what is likely to happen in the future. For example, it is possible to assess the risk of a forest fire occurring a certain area using historical temperature, humidity, rainfall patterns, and actual incidents of forest fires. If we extend that concept a little, we can see ways to make use of these predictive tools in enterprise resource planning. One requirements that has come up frequently in client organizations is the ability to forecast future demand for products. Today, it's more art than it is science.

We've observed that, in many situations, the forecast is optimistic based upon the Sales team's projections. Similarly, executives of the company have an overly rosy view of what's going to happen in the future. The forecast then drives MRP to recommend purchasing more material than the operations team actually needs. This increases inventory carrying costs as a result. The other side of the issue is not having enough inventory. In these situations, shipments may be delayed due to being out of stock of key component materials. The forecasting methodology can be refined in such a way where it's optimized to minimize inventory carrying costs and the opportunity cost of lost sales due to "out of stock" situations. The forecast can be self-correcting and, if in error, can be adjusted based on actual demand. This will serve to reduce the production of finished goods and the ordering of component raw materials. The entire MRP shifts as the sales forecast is adjusted. Artificial intelligence can be inserted into the process so that sales forecasting is significantly more accurate. This creates a number of opportunities. For example, in addition to historical sales of products, macroeconomic, social media and publicly available can be included in the forecasting algorithm. The resulting models can then generate even more accurate forecasts.

Here are some possible data elements that might be used to predict customer demand:

- Historical sales by month

- Trends year to year

- Seasonality

- Overall industry demand

- Social media chatter related to the product or product category

- Publicly available data

  - Industry associations

  - Government agencies

  - Academic studies

Augmented Reality

Another set of innovations have become popular in recent years. They can be called artificial intelligence to some extent, but deserve their own classification. These are virtual reality, augmented reality, and mixed reality. Here's how to distinguish them:

Virtual reality (VR)	3 dimensional images Human interaction • Helmet with screen • Gloves with sensors
Augmented reality (AR)	View of the real world Superimposes computer generated images Composite view
Mixed reality (MR)	A form of augmented reality Somewhere between VR and AR View of the real world Superimposes virtual objects that also appear to be real

We encountered an interesting example of augmented reality in the construction industry. When constructing a building, having virtual access to the blueprints and data on what still needed to be constructed can be very valuable. In this example, the developer was able to apply augmented reality to the construction of a commercial building. Construction workers, wearing headsets, were able to complete construction tasks with visual cues. They put framing, electrical, and plumbing components in the right places without having to refer to the blueprints. It was all visually in front of them, available through augmented reality.

Augmented reality opens doors to other opportunities within business organizations. Imagine training employees in a manufacturing or production facility. With augmented reality, clients can do that in a virtual world and begin to elevate the skill sets of machine operators. Supervisors can show production personnel exactly what they need to be doing in an augmented view rather than having to take time on (or off) the production floor for conventional training. There are a lot of opportunities in this area in manufacturing organizations and service organizations. Historically, teaching production personnel how to complete complex tasks has been a major endeavor. Being able to do that in a virtual world would enable manufacturing and services organizations to bring people up to speed quickly and conserve financial resources.

Headsets

Envision having shop floor personnel with augmented reality readily available to them through headsets with audio, video, natural language processing, and speech synthesis. They will have all of the information necessary to assemble the parts and be able to transmit all of the production order information for the ERP application with one hands-free device. Web-enabled cameras can capture video and images of the production process to help identify errors. Built-in microphones and natural language processing can facilitate the process of data capture for the ERP application. Built-in speakers will provide the ability to quickly communicate with supervisors and co-workers. The bulky headsets available today will be replaced by conventional-looking eyeglasses or safety glasses.

Some of the technology we described in this chapter might sound like something out of a science fiction movie. However, here we are today with these capabilities now becoming part of everyday life. Some of the things that General Electric has already implemented in some of their heavy production is truly innovative. Many of these technologies are already being utilized at the Fortune 500 level. We expect that they will, within a relatively short time frame, trickle down to small and medium-sized businesses as well.

FINAL THOUGHTS

In Summary

In Chapter 1, we reviewed selecting an ERP application. In situations where an industry-specific application is available, it should be considered. Company size, fit with existing manufacturing processes, and technology infrastructure should be considered in the software selection process.

In Chapter 2, we reviewed implementation cost and timing. Hardware, software, and consulting costs are pretty easy identify. Estimating the internal costs, specifically human resources, if sometimes more difficult. The overall cost of the implementation should be weighed against the expected benefits. Underestimating the time to implement has a number of adverse ramifications, including the possibility of selecting a sub-optimal set of resources for the implementation.

In Chapter 3, we reviewed migrating the data from the old to the new application. Ultimately the client has the responsibility for the integrity of the data. Selecting which data to migrate (i.e., master data, open transactions, transaction history) will directly influence the cost of the data migration. There is an opportunity to clean up the data in the process of data migration. A data warehouse may be helpful in the process of data migration and providing a repository for the data in the old system.

In Chapter 4, we reviewed the activities typically executed in an ERP system implementation. These activities span planning, business process analysis, business process reengineering, training, and documentation. One of the more important activities is pilot testing since errors in data migration or transaction processing procedures will have a significant impact when the organization goes live on the new system.

In Chapter 5, we covered common issues that arise during an ERP system implementation. These include significant changes in scope, problems with the data migration, and unexpected demands on internal personnel. One of the most impactful issues is not having adequate change management processes in place during the implementation.

In Chapter 6, we outlined reasons to engage a consulting resource to support the implementation. Insufficient internal resources, a steep learning curve, and total cost of ownership are primary factors. Also, a consulting firm can help to shorten the implementation time allowing the client organization to realize a return on investment more quickly than it otherwise would have.

In Chapter 7, we reviewed ways to manage the data in the old system. Keeping the old system operational and loading data from the old system into a data warehouse are common solutions. One key consideration is the platform the old system is running on. Maintaining a current platform (e.g., Windows / SQL) is much simpler than maintaining something older (e.g., UNIX / BISAM).

In Chapter 8, we reviewed the pros and cons of custom software development. The 80 / 20 rule applies in that 80% of the functionality needed should be the standard software. Leveraging third-party applications and built-in APIs are preferable to developing custom software. Automating sub-optimal business processes with custom software development should only be undertaken as a last resort.

In Chapter 9, we covered user adoption of the new ERP system. In general, I/T cannot complete the implementation on its own. It takes a village. Training, documentation, and transfer of knowledge are key activities that increase user adoption. Finance should be involved at the beginning of the implementation rather than the end to ensure that inventory control and production transactions impact the G/L correctly.

In Chapter 10, we covered common post-implementation issues. Underestimating scope, cost, and timing are the most common. One of the more subtle issues implementing phases that are too large. Taking an agile approach and implementing smaller phases allows clients to get a faster return on investment as phases are implemented within the organization.

In Chapter 11, we reviewed the Internet of Things and how it applies to ERP. With sensors and business analytics, systems can predict when equipment is about to fail. This provides maintenance personnel the opportunity to replace a failing component and minimize downtime. Real-time location tracking can be employed to monitor the location of assets in motion within and outside the manufacturing facility.

In Chapter 12, we reviewed artificial intelligence and how it applies to ERP. Business analytics and managing big data are basic requirements. Supply chain management and sales forecasting are key opportunities. Augmented reality, coupled with artificial intelligence, could significantly improve the financial metrics in manufacturing firms.

What's next?

Let's take look at the future prospects for ERP planning applications.

Cloud Applications

We see the shift to cloud computing continuing to improve the cost-effectiveness of ERP applications. The cloud is the more sensible approach in the long-run. Many organizations have made large investments in server hardware and then utilized a relatively small fraction of its capabilities. Today, clients can effectively "rent" that functionality in a cloud model, sharing computing resources with other organizations. The result is that the physical hardware itself is getting a much higher level of utilization as virtual machines are provisioned on it. So, for the foreseeable future, the shift to the cloud will continue.

As of this writing, established manufacturing organizations seem to be hesitant to move their hardware and software off-premises or into the cloud. Many I/T executives have been resistant in that they prefer to keep everything on-premises, perhaps for control. In some exceptional cases, mostly large companies, I/T is very well-developed. These organizations have lots of personnel, large server rooms, good electrical power, fast Internet connections, air conditioning, and redundancy. From that standpoint, these firms can do many things on-premises. Smaller organizations generally cannot support that kind of infrastructure and are better candidates to pursue a cloud solution for their ERP applications.

The hybrid model for I/T infrastructure is becoming more common. In these cases, a portion is kept on-premises and a portion resides in the cloud. We see the initial steps to implement cloud backup and disaster recovery. Secondary functions might be migrated into the cloud keeping the primary operation on-premises. As time goes on, more and more will get pushed into the cloud and, at some point, cloud computing be the de facto standard.

Artificial Intelligence

Some of the other things that we've covered, including the Internet of Things, and the connectedness of devices and software will provide executives with better and more timely information to conduct analyses and make decisions. We see this trend continuing and growing exponentially as organizations are presented with more and more information. We are already seeing that today as businesses are generating and capturing data from various sources. That doesn't necessarily make it easier for humans to make decisions. This is one of the challenges and opportunities for artificial intelligence. At some point, we may find that the human brain just can't make sense of all of that data. However, a machine can. It can consolidate the information and present options with corresponding probabilities based on the available data.

Machines can do the heavy lifting, processing the data and painting a picture of what may be happening. Whether it is labor data collected on the shop floor, financial performance indicators, or data from the human resources information system, consolidation of these massive quantities of data will, at some point, become a major challenge for humans. We also foresee a shift to faster, smarter machines. It will be an evolution rather than an overnight occurrence. If Google can enable cars that drive themselves, imagine what can be accomplished using similar intelligence in a manufacturing environment.

Salesforce.com recently announced the introduction of Einstein, an artificial intelligence component of its well-known software as a service (SaaS) sales automation platform. We think that this will be more common as software applications get rolled out. These applications will simply end up having an AI component built into them. Sometime, in the not-so-distant future, there is going to be

AI functionality built into ERP applications. The AI will help with the processing and interpretation of transactions and decision-making in manufacturing organizations.

We briefly touched on the opportunity to go and grab data from outside the organization. Historically, ERP applications have been focused on internal sales and purchase order processing, financial reporting, inventory control, and manufacturing. However, there are some interesting external sources of data that might be useful to merge into the ERP application. This includes the Internet of Things data mentioned earlier. Other types of external data include geographic, demographic, and psychographic, some of which might be useful in the ERP application.

Machines Manufacturing Machines

The term "lights out manufacturing" refers to situations in which a manufacturing facility can operate with little or no human presence. People are required for the preparation of component materials, receipt of finished goods, and quality assurance. Opportunities for hybrid scenarios exist in which one process or one shift could be "lights out". The term automatic factory applies to situations where there is little or no human intervention. For example, FANUC, a Japanese robotics manufacturer, uses robots to manufacture robots at a rate of about 50 per day. Not only are the lights turned off, but the heating and air conditioning as well. It seems like something out of science fiction, however, it's happening today in advanced manufacturing facilities. Machines making machines is a little bit unnerving, however, they are a long way from taking over the world.

Losing Jobs to Automation

One of the challenges is that the U.S. has lost more jobs to automation than to offshore competitors. If current trends continue, job losses will expand rapidly. So, what does the future hold? Many of the innovations we've talked about involve replacing people, which is good for business. Is there a point at which to strike a balance? If a machine can run 24 x 7 x 365 with a relatively low maintenance requirement and it can replace a human operator, why would an organization not automate if it was cost-effective? These are macroeconomic and geopolitical issues that are outside of our areas of expertise, however, we are already seeing it happening.

###

We hope that this book has been helpful to you and that you've enjoyed reading it as much as we've enjoyed writing it. We are always happy to help others using what we've learned and would like to offer a way to continue our conversation.

A special offer for who those have purchased this book

As a thank you for purchasing our book, we are offering a **free** 3-part course titled, "Discovery, Diagnosis, and Business Process Analysis in Enterprise Resource Planning". In this course, we will expand on some of the concepts in this book and provide related tools to leverage the utilization of an ERP application. This $250 value is provided to you at *no charge*.

To register, go to http://bit.ly/2wRaFVM

83900437R00066

Made in the USA
Lexington, KY
16 March 2018